For my Wifey Cassie, who is mental enough with

And our adorable, loving and amazing Godchildre
missed so much throughout this madness of the lockdown of 2020

Jake, Zac, Leoni & Junior

Love you all

Mr J (jay jay)

Once upon a time in a land of semi normal state

The year started fine without no real knowing stake

But as news started about a global virus

A lot ignored thinking it would never find us

But as more people got sick and sadly left the world

Our leaders thought of rules that twisted and twirled

Confusion got made when toilet rolls got hit

Hey, if I'm locked in I'll need that to …. Sneeze

As shopping became crazy and shelves become bare

We forgot about others, we forgot how to care

As I sat here with wifey locked in our home

Shaving my head so I needed no comb

We missed our godchildren who came round to bake

I thought I know I'll share virtual cake

I turned to my book of faces and started to share

Then people followed and started to care

Families baked and shared their love

I forgot to pre warn you'll need an oven glove

So as months passed and bans got lifted

We understood that our families are gifted

We cuddled and played in our own prison cell

But filled it with love and a cinnamon smell

So let's not forget what we have learnt

Turn off the Netflix or your buns will get burnt

So as we prepare for the new world rules put in fashion

Please just never lose your passion

Mr J

xxx

WELCOME

HERE ARE THE RULES FOR BAKERS BIG OR SMALL

HAVE FUN WITH OTHERS GIVE SOMEONE A CALL

FIRST WASH YOUR HANDS, AND GIVE THEM A SCRUB

NO ONE WANTS DIRT WHEN YOU'RE DISHING OUT GRUB

GET YOUR INGRIEDIENTS AND EQUIPMENT READY

YOU MAY NEED SOME GLOVES IF YOUR FINGERS GET BREADY

CLEAN AS YOU GO AND TRY TO KEEP TIDY

OR YOU'LL GET TOLD OFF AND HAVE NOTHING TO BITEY

THE MAIN THING TO DO IS HAVE BAKING FUN

UNLESS IT'S NICE OUTSIDE THEN GO AND ENJOY THE SUN

I WISH YOU ALL WELL AND ENJOY THE BOOK

GO ON NOW START HAVING A LOOK

CONTENTS

No page numbers, I like the game of chance just open up and take your luck.

Dairy free bakes are noted in this book but for gluten free you can replace the flour with a suitable gluten free substitute along with a gluten free baking powder

CHOCOLATE CHIP COOKIES

you will need

225g soft unsalted butter or Dairy free margarine
110g caster sugar
275g plain flour
75g chocolate chips

If you don't want to add chocolate chips maybe a teaspoon of either cinnamon, ginger or mixed spice.

A mixing bowl
A sieve
A baking tray with either grease proof paper or lightly dusted with flour.

Preheat your oven to 180C/GM 4.

Sieve your flour into your bowl and add the butter, gently rub the mix between your fingers to form an even crumbly mix. If you are using a spice instead of chocolate chips you should add this now.

Add your sugar and continue to mix until it's all evenly combined.

Start to firmly knead your mixture together to create a huge cookie dough ball, you might need to add a little milk or vanilla essence to help you but you should be fine.

Now add your chocolate chips and quickly fold this evenly into your dough mix, we didn't do this earlier as we don't want sweaty choc chips,

Now with your mix you need to start making little balls about the size of a walnut, so tear away bits from your cookie dough and get rolling in the palm of your hands, make sure they are all equal in size.

Place these onto your greased or lined baking sheet and with two fingers gently press them down to form a nice round thickish looking biscuit just under a cm

Pop into your preheated oven and check after 10 minutes they should need around 10-15 but never forget to have a sneaky peak to see how they are doing.

Once done remove from oven and allow to cool either on the tray or on a wire rack.

SHORTBREAD BISCUITS

You will need

125g Unsalted butter or dairy free alternative
55g caster sugar
180g plain flour
1 teaspoon of vanilla essence (optional)
Some cold water

A mixing bowl
A sieve
Rolling pin

Preheat Oven to 180C/GM 4

Sieve your flour then add your sugar and butter and gently rub the mixture together with your fingers binding the ingredients until it's a breadcrumb style mix.

Add the vanilla and a little cold water to the mix and continue to mix until you have a smooth dough adding a little water at a time as you need it.

If using a dairy free alternative I suggest rolling the mix into a log, cling film and refrigerate or freeze to firm your mix up before cutting ,

On a lightly floured work top roll out the dough to about the thickness of a pencil.

Cut into even shapes and dot with a fork to allow even cooking.

Bake for 10-15 minutes or until firm but still pale, Dust with a little extra sugar whilst cooling

BANANA & CHOCOLATE CHIP (or blueberry) MUFFINS

You will need

3 ripe bananas
110g caster sugar
50g melted unsalted butter or Dairy free alternative
170g Self raising flour
I teaspoon baking powder
110g plain chocolate chips or blueberries

A mixing bowl
A sieve
Muffin tray
Muffin cases
Potato masher (optional)

Pre heat oven 180C/GM 4

Add the peeled bananas, sugar and melted butter into a bowl and mash together, you could use a potato masher or wearing gloves or clean hands to squish this all together, but go crazy until it is lump free, tiny bits of banana are fine you won't be able to get it perfectly lump free.

Then sieve in your flour and baking soda and gently fold in the mixture to an even batter style mix.

Add your chocolate chips or blueberries depending on if you wish to be naughty or nice and combine well into the mixture until evenly mixed.

Divide the mix between your muffin cases that you will have placed into your muffin tray, make sure your mix is even by placing one spoonful of mix at a time into each muffin case.

Pop these beauties into your preheated oven for around 15 minutes, they should be firm yet spongey to the touch, you won't get a clean knife test on these as they will get gooey chocolate or blueberry juice on the test.

Allow to cool and enjoy.

GINGERBREAD RECIPE

You will need

350g Plain flour + extra for rolling out later
1 teaspoon bicarbonate of soda
2 teaspoons ground ginger
1 teaspoon ground cinnamon
175g light brown soft sugar
125g unsalted butter or Dairy free alternative
1 egg
4 tablespoons golden syrup

A mixing bowl
A sieve
A mixing spoon
A rolling pin
Biscuit cutters of any shape

Preheat the oven 180C/GM 4

Sieve your flour then add your bicarbonate of soda, ginger, cinnamon and then your softened butter.

Get rubbing until you get that breadcrumb style mix.

Add your sugar and mix in together, make a little well in the centre of your mix and then add your egg and golden syrup. Using a spoon gently combine the mix together after a while you'll need to get your hands in there to give a good old clump together as this should now be forming a firm ball of gingerbread.

Tip the gingerbread ball onto your work top and shape it into a block, cling film your gingerbread block and refrigerate for about 20 minutes.

Once chilled remove from fridge, lightly flour your worktop area and the gingerbread block and your rolling pin,

Gently and evenly roll your gingerbread block out to about 1/2 cm thickness, cut into your desired shapes and re-roll any leftover mix again to make more biscuits.

Place your biscuits onto your lined baking trays and bake at 180/GM 4 for about 12-15 minutes or until golden and mildly firm, remove from oven and allow to cool on the baking trays, whilst cooling you can add chocolate chip eyes or with a cocktail stick gently draw a smiley face and buttons.

CHEESE SCONES

You will need

250g self-raising flour
Pinch of salt
Teaspoon of either cayenne pepper, paprika, chives, mustard or poppy seeds
1 teaspoon of baking powder
75g butter
120g grated cheddar cheese
80-90 ml milk
Extra cheese for topping the scones

A mixing bowl
A sieve
Baking tray
Round cutter (optional)

Preheat your oven 180C/GM 4

Firstly sieve your flour into your mixing bowl then add your butter and gently rub together to form a crumb like mix.

Add your salt, baking powder and any additional seasoning that you desired from the ingredients and then add your grated cheese.

Mix and combine it all together then slowly add a little bit of milk, continue to mix until you have a lovely doughy ball.

Lightly flour your worktop and your rolling pin and roll out to about 2cm deep and using your cutter cut as many scones as you can before re-rolling and doing the same again.

Or as per the cookie recipe you could roll the mix with your hands into ball shapes and then gently flatten giving you a more rustic looking scone.

Place onto your lined baking sheet and place into your pre heated oven for 10 minutes, after that you need to remove them from the oven and sprinkle each scone with a little extra cheese and give them a further 5 minutes.

Once done you can allow to cool but these beauties are best served fresh and warm with a lovely spread of butter gently melting into them.

FRUIT SCONES

You will need

115 g softened butter
225 g self raising flour
15 g caster sugar
3 tablespoons milk
30 g dried fruit either sultanas, raisins soaked in cold tea for 10 minutes

A mixing bowl
A sieve
Rolling pin and round cutter (optional)
Baking tray

Pre heat oven 180C?GM4

Sieve your flour, add your butter and get rubbing with that mix between your fingers until it looks like breadcrumbs.

Add your sugar and give it another little mix. Add your drained fruit add a little milk and start to combine your mix together, slowly add the rest of the milk until you have a firm scone dough ball.

Lightly flour your worktop and your rolling pin and roll out to about 2cm deep and using your cutter cut as many scones as you can before re-rolling and doing the same again.

Like the cheese scone recipe you can ball the mixture up onto your baking sheet, gently flattening the tops with 2 fingers.

Brush the tops with a little bit of milk.

Bake for 20-25 minutes on 180/GM4 and serve with butter, cream or jam or all of it if you have it.

ROCKY ROAD

You will need

500g milk or dark chocolate
30g mini marshmallows
30g breakfast cereal (cornflakes or Cheerios are the best)
30g chopped dried fruit (cherries, apricots, and banana whatever you may have)
100g Butter
4 tablespoons of golden syrup
30g sultanas, raisins, or currants
2 crushed biscuits - anything you like or have
1 packet of mini eggs or 2 chocolate bars of your choice broken up

A saucepan big enough for the above
A mixing spoon
A cake tin either round or square 8-10 inch lined with grease proof paper

Melt the butter and golden syrup gently in a saucepan

Add the chocolate and continue to stir until it has all melted

Pour the rest of the ingredients in apart from your seasonal or chosen style of topping

Gently fold the mixture together ensuring the ingredients are thoroughly covered in your chocolate mixture

Pour your mixture into your lined cake tin and spread and level using the back of your spoon

Spread about your chosen topping, I used mini eggs as it was Easter, you can break chocolate bars up and make it look rustic and gently press them into your rocky mix then refrigerate until set. Once cooled remove from the cake tin and cut into the desired portion size you require, store in an air proof container and store in a cool area.

COCONUT MACAROONS

You will need

4 egg whites
200g caster sugar
300g desiccated coconut
Some chocolate to melt for decorating

A mixing bowl
A mixing spoon
A biscuit cutter
A lined baking tray

Pre heat your oven to 180C/GM 4

In a mixing bowl place your egg whites, keep the yolks in the fridge you may use them for something later in the day.

Give your whites a quick whisk, not too much just so it's a bit frothy.

Add your sugar and coconut to your frothy egg white and give it a good mix until it starts to clump together.

With your biscuit/pastry cutter take a spoonful of your mix and place it in the cutter, gently press the mix down, your macaroons need to be about 2cm deep. It's easier to do this on the baking sheet so you don't have to move them about.

Continue to do this with all of your mixture.

Place in your pre heated oven for 12-15 minutes until they gently start to colour but not too much.

Once cooked allow to cool fully on your baking tray, once cooled decorate with melted chocolate and allow the chocolate to naturally set.

CARROT CAKE MUFFINS (makes 12)

You will need

150g melted margarine
250g grated carrot
200g caster sugar
200g Self raising flour
2 teaspoons cinnamon
2 teaspoons baking powder
2 eggs
125g sultanas (optional)

A mixing bowl
A sieve
A mixing spoon
12 muffin cases
Muffin trays either 2x6 or 1x12

Preheat oven 180C/GM4

Wash, peel and top and tail your carrots and grate for the correct amount.

Melt margarine in microwave and add to your mixing bowl.

Add grated carrot and sugar to your margarine and stir.

Once evenly mixed sieve in your flour, cinnamon and baking powder.

Add your eggs.

Add sultanas if you wish

Give another really good mix until all combined.

Divide the mix between the 12 muffin cases

Bake in the oven for around 20-25 minutes allow to cool, you can make a carrot cake icing by mixing 100g icing sugar and 50g softened butter until pale then add 100g soft cream cheese. Blend together then either pipe or spread over your muffins, for an extra zing grate a zest of an orange over the iced muffins.

VANILLA CUPCAKES

You will need

150g butter (very soft not melted)
150g sugar
150g self raising flour
2 eggs
2 teaspoons of vanilla essence

A mixing bowl
A whisk
A sieve
6 muffin cases of 12 smaller cupcake cases
Muffin or cupcake tray

Preheat oven 180C/GM 4

Add your butter and sugar and whisk, whisk away as these 2 ingredients need to be creamed together so they are almost white in colour.

Add 1 egg and sieve half your flour in.

Gently ... And I mean gently using the whisk mix together to start making your cake mix.

Add your second egg and remaining flour and gently mix again.

Add your vanilla essence and gently mix again.

Divide your mix between 6 muffin cases or 12 cupcake cases

Bake for 10-15 minutes 180/ gm4

Once done, allow to cool and decorate using whatever you have. If you want a simple buttercream icing simply weigh some icing sugar out then add half the amount of butter (i.e. 100g icing / 50g butter) whisk together you can add food colouring if you wish, then sprinkles once the been put the buttercream on your cakes.

BASIC FLAPJACK RECIPE

You will need

300g porridge oats
150g butter
150g light brown sugar (caster if you have no other)
2-3 tablespoons golden syrup

This can have fruit or nuts added to it all you need to do is remove 50g -75g oats and replace with 50-75g of fruit or nuts or a mixture of both depending on how fruity or nutty you like it

An 8inch square tin lined with greaseproof
A saucepan
A spoon
Baking tray

Pre heat your oven 180C/ GM 4

On a baking tray pour on your oats and crushed nuts if you are using any, and gently toast these off in your oven before you do anything else. Once done remove and set aside.

In a large saucepan big enough for all your ingredients add your butter add slowly on a low heat start to melt, add your sugar and golden syrup. Turn up the heat a little more and continue to stir until it's gently bubbling but not burning or caramelising.

Add in your toasted oats and if you are adding fruit or nuts these can go in with your oats and fold the mixture together so your mix is evenly coated, at this point you can add a little spice such as ginger which is wonderful in a flapjack.

Spoon your mix into your lined tin and spread out evenly gently pushing the mix down to make it level.

Place into your oven for 20-25 minutes , you can tell it is ready because it will be slightly firm on the top but be careful checking as this is very sugary and hot, hot, hot.

Leave to cool to ensure it doesn't break up before removing it from the tin but once it has cooled you can then portion your flapjack into bars or bite sized pieces to enjoy.

CUSTARD CREAMS

You will need

170g softened butter
170g self raising flour
55g icing sugar
55g custard powder (not instant powder)

FOR THE FILLING

70g softened butter
70g icing sugar
70g custard powder (not instant powder)

A mixing bowl
A sieve
A lined baking tray
A rolling pin
A wooden spoon or spatula
A knife or biscuit cutter

Preheat your oven to 180C/GM4

Cream together your softened butter and icing sugar best to use a wooden spoon or plastic spatula for this, once creamed you can sieve in your flour and custard powder. Using your hands get this mixture into a nice big ball of biscuity goodness once done lightly dust your work surface and your rolling pin and your biscuit ball and gently roll out to about just under 1/2 cm.
Now you can either trim the edges to make a traditional square biscuit or use a cutter to just make sure they are all the same size cut as many as you can and then place them onto a lined baking sheet leaving a good gap in between each biscuit, with a fork gently press on each biscuit to give a slight pattern effect.
Now bake in your pre heated oven 180 / gm 4 for about 10-12 minutes once done they should be light in colour but firm to the touch. Whilst your biscuits are baking lets   on with the creamy filling, add your filling ingredients to a mixing bowl and with a spoon or spatula I need you to cream these ingredients together to a good paste.

Take one biscuit and on the unmarked side pipe or spread your filling evenly and then sandwich with another biscuit then continue with the rest…. You're done

COCONUT ICE

You will need

250g sweetened condensed milk
250g icing sugar + extra for dusting
200g desiccated coconut
Red or pink food colouring or others to make it your own crazy recipe ☺

A mixing bowl
A sieve
A mixing spoon

Let's make sure you've washed your hands you might have to get your hands in with this.

Right let's sieve that icing sugar into your mixing bowl.

Pour your measured amount of sweetened condensed milk in with your icing sugar and gently start to mix together.

Add your coconut and then combine together.... this is where you can start to work this with your hands ... you should end up with a firm ball that's just a little sticky but not too much.

Divide your ball into 2, set one ball aside and with the half in your mixing bowl add a little bit of red of pink food colouring, if you want to do multiple colours divide the mix into the amount of colours you would like.

Once mixed and the colour is even I need you to lightly dust your worktop with a sprinkling of icing sugar.

Get your mix one ball at a time and shape it into a square or rectangle shape that are both equal in size.

Lay one on top of the other and gently tap around the top and the sides to seal together.

Cling film and refrigerate for at least 3 hours then once done cut into your required bite size treats

JAMMY DODGERS

You will need

For the biscuit

175g unsalted butter or dairy free alt
250g Plain flour + a little for dusting later
100g icing sugar
1 egg yolk

For the filling

250g icing sugar
100g soft unsalted butter
Some jam or lemon curd

A mixing bowl
A sieve
A rolling pin
A biscuit cutter
A small circular cutter
2 lined baking trays
PRE HEAT OVEN 180C/ GM4

Firstly sieve your flour and icing sugar then add your butter, now rub the butter and flour/sugar between your fingers until the mixture is well blended this won't be like fine breadcrumbs as it has been with previous recipes so don't worry, its fine

Add your egg yolk and get your hands in there and give it a good mix we need a big ball of dodger mix

Lightly flour your work top and the dodger ball and your rolling pin you need to gently roll out your mix to just under 1/2 cm

With your biscuit cutter cut as many biscuits as you can, but we need an even amount

Place even amounts of your biscuits between your 2 trays, place 1 tray in the oven for 10 - 15 minutes that should have been pre heated to 180/ gm 4

With the other tray using a smaller cutter or as i am using a piping nozzle cut a hole in the centre of your remaining tray of biscuits.

Once your first tray of biscuits is done remove and allow to cool then place your other tray of biscuits in to cook for between 10-15 minutes they should be light in colour but firm.

Whilst one trays cooling and the other tray is cooking let's make the filling, sieve your icing sugar into a mixing bowl and add your butter and blend together to a stiff paste.

Gently pipe your butter icing around your biscuit leaving a space in the middle for your jam

Add your biscuit with a cut hole on top of your biscuit with icing and jam and gently press down, not too hard and there you go.

CHOCOLATE AND RASPBERRY BROWNIES

You will need

200g dark chocolate
100g milk chocolate
250g unsalted butter
400g soft light brown sugar
4 large eggs
150g plain flour
50g cocoa powder
200g raspberries
White chocolate to decorate (optional)

A saucepan
A wooden spoon or plastic spatula
A sieve
2 lined square 8in tins OR a roasting tray roughly 20 x 30 cm

Pre heat your oven 180C/GM 4

Place your butter, sugar and chocolate in a saucepan and gently melt on a moderate heat, stirring occasionally, remove from the heat and let cool for just a couple of minutes.

Add one egg at a time into your melted chocolate mix and mix well, after your second egg has been added, sieve half the amount of your flour into the mix.

After adding the remaining 2 eggs, sieve the remaining flour and the cocoa powder.

Add half the amount of raspberries to your mix, stirring to break the raspberries down.

Spread your mix evenly between your 2 tins or the larger one if you have it.
Bake on the middle shelf of your preheated oven for 30-35 minutes, until your top is firm.
Once cooked remove from oven and allow to cool,

You now have the option of decorating your brownie with the additional raspberries and melting down white chocolate over them.

RASPBERRY & WHITE CHOCOLATE BLONDIES

You will need

200g soft butter
200g caster sugar
3 medium eggs
150g plain flour
1 teaspoon vanilla essence
175g white chocolate chips
150g raspberries

Decoration optional
Dusting of icing sugar or melted white chocolate
A mixing bowl
An 8in square cake tin
A sieve
An electric whisk or a hand whisk and some muscles.

Preheat your oven to 180C/GM 4

Melt the butter in a bowl in a microwave and put to one side.

In a bowl I need you to whisk together the sugar eggs and vanilla essence,. this needs to be whisked until light and fluffy and doubled in volume ... so that's why I advised an electric whisk.

Once your egg/sugar mix is done I need you to slowly add the butter a spoonful at a time then mix in well ... be patient this may take a while.

Once all your butter is in you can now sieve in your flour and gently start to fold the mixture together.

Once that's done you can now add your white chocolate chips and raspberries and fold them in together.

Pour your mix into your baking tin and place into your preheated oven and bake for around 35/40 minutes once you think it's done check with a knife or skewer to make sure ... it needs to come out of the Blondie all clear and not sticky.

Allow to cool in the tin, once cooled you can either dust with icing sugar or drizzle a little more white chocolate over, once cooled portion off and enjoy

JAFFA DRIZZLE CAKE

You will need

140g butter softened
200g self-raising flour
11/2 tsp baking powder
200g golden caster sugar
3 large eggs
6 tbsp milk
Finely grated zest 1 large orange

To finish

3 tbsp orange juice
50g golden caster sugar
50g dark chocolate

A mixing bowl
A hand or electric whisk
A loaf tin greased and lined

Preheat oven to 180C/GM4

Butter and line the base of a standard loaf tin. Put all the cake ingredients into a bowl and beat with a hand whisk or wooden spoon for 3-5 minutes, until light and fluffy. Spoon the mix into the tin and level the top.

Bake for 40-50 minutes, until golden brown and firm to the touch. Meanwhile, heat the orange juice and sugar gently in a small pan, stirring until dissolved. When the cake is cooked, remove it from the oven and spoon over the orange mix. Leave to cool in the tin, then remove and cool completely on a wire rack.

Break up the chocolate into a bowl and melt over a pan of simmering water or in the microwave on Medium for 1-2 minutes drizzle over the cake and leave to set.

STICKY GINGER CAKE

You will need

100g butter or margarine
100g dark brown sugar
180g golden syrup
2 eggs, lightly beaten
175g self-raising flour
4 tsp ground ginger
1 teaspoon mixed spice

A mixing bowl
A sieve
A mixing spoon
A cake tin 8" round or square lined with great proof paper

Preheat your oven to 180C/GM 4

Cream the butter and sugar together you'll need a little bit longer than usual as we are using dark brown sugar which is a little denser and heavier than caster we used in previous recipes

Once it's a good creamy texture add the golden syrup and gently fold together.

Add your eggs and slowly start to sieve your flour, ginger and mixed spice.

No need to be that gentle giving this mix a final whizz as it's going to be a mix of a sponge but still a sticky cake, but it won't have the dark traditional stickiness of a Jamaican cake as we didn't use black treacle as in traditional recipes.

Pour mix into lined 8" tin ... square would be good but rounds fine.

Place your bake into your preheated oven for around 25-30 minutes.

The bake may look likes getting over done.... stay calm .... it's got syrup that's going to be cooking real hot.... remove when it's just firm to the touch and allow to cool in the tin at allow to maintain its moisture and stickiness.

Cut and serve and enjoy.

BANANA & PECAN TEABREAD

You will need

4 ripe bananas
125g soft unsalted butter or DF margarine
175g caster sugar
2 eggs
2 tablespoons golden syrup
225g self raising flour
75g pecan nuts (walnuts if you fancy them instead)

A mixing bowl
A mixing spoon
A sieve
A lightly greased or lined loaf tin

Preheat oven 180C/GM 4

In your mixing bowl cream together your sugar and butter until it is light and pasty looking.
Add your ripe bananas to the sugar and butter mixture and mix in well so there's no lumpy bits of banana,
Add your golden syrup, eggs and gently sieve your flour into the mix, if you fancy at this point you could put a small pinch of cinnamon into the mix to give it a kick

Stir the mix well making sure everything is combined.

Pour the mix into your loaf tin, once it's all in the tin give it a gentle wiggle to make sure it's all level then arrange the pecan nuts on the top.

As I stated in the ingredients you can use walnuts instead if you fancy.

Place in the middle of your preheated oven and bake for 1hour - 1hour 15 minutes until it is firm to the touch.

Once done allow to cool in the tin. Once cooled slice and enjoy.

This can be toasted the next day and enjoy with a spoonful of honey spread over it or a Nutella/ chocolate spread.

VICTORIA SPONGE

You will need

250g caster sugar
250g unsalted butter or Dairy free alternative
250g Self raising flour
4 eggs
2 tablespoons of vanilla essence

For the filling

100g unsalted butter or Dairy free alternative
180g icing sugar
Strawberry or raspberry jam (optional)

2 8inch round cake tins, greased and lined
A mixing bowl
A whisk
A sieve
A spoon or spatula
Preheat your oven 180c/GM4

In your mixing bowl you need to add your butter and sugar and using a whisk cream together until pale and creamy.

Gradually start to add one egg at a time and a little of your sieved flour and gently fold together, continue to do this until you've used the eggs and flour up, now you can add your vanilla essence and stir well, you should have a smooth cake like thick batter.

Divide your mixture evenly between your 2 lined cake tins and with a spatula or back of a spoon level your mix off.

Place into your preheated oven for 20-25 minutes until golden and springy to the touch, you can use a sharp knife to ensure the middle is done if you wish.

Allow to cool for 5-10 minutes before removing them from their tins and allow to cool further.

Whilst they are cooling you can make the buttercream by whisking together the butter and icing sugar.
Once your cakes are cooled you can on one cake spread a layer of your chosen jam and pipe your buttercream on top of your jam and then top with your other cake layer, Lightly dust with some icing sugar and there you go.

THE PUFFIN (pizza muffins)

You will need

175g plain flour
1 teaspoon baking powder
1/2 teaspoon bicarbonate of soda
100ml vegetable oil
50ml milk
75g grated cheese
Salt & pepper
2 rashers of lean bacon
6 slices pepperoni or chorizo
1 spring onion
To top the muffins a tomato sauce/ salsa or as I've used a tomato style pesto and some grated cheese

A muffin tin and 6 muffin cases
A mixing bowl
A sieve

Preheat your oven to 180C/GM 4

In your mixing bowl sieve your flower, add your baking powder, bicarbonate of soda and season well with salt and pepper.

Add your milk and oil and mix well, don't panic but this will form a sticky dough rather than the muffin mixes you're used to.

Finely chop your bacon, pepperoni and spring onion.

Add the cheese and your chopped ingredients to your muffin dough and using your hands mix the ingredients well so that the mix looks even.

Divide the mix into 6 equal balls and place into your muffin cases. Bake in your preheated oven for around 20 minutes.

Just before they are ready remove from oven and spread your tomato topping on and then sprinkle some extra cheese on top and give another couple of minutes to melt in the oven

Serve with a garlic mayo or tomato salsa dip and enjoy.

BASIC GARLIC & HERB FOCACCIA

You will need

100ml olive oil
2 cloves of garlic, chopped
1 tablespoon of dried herbs (your choice basil, oregano, thyme etc.)
Salt and pepper
200ml warm water
2 1/2 teaspoons active dried yeast
1/2 teaspoon of honey
350g plain flour

A mixing bowl
A sieve
A warm place to proof your bread
A roasting tray
Preheat your oven to 180C/GM 4

In a jug get your measured warm water add your yeast and your honey and leave for 5 minutes.

Sieve your flour into your bowl, add ¾ of your olive oil to your flour and add your chopped garlic.

Slowly start to pour into your flour bowl the warm yeast liquid you made earlier and gradually start to work your mix until it forms a dough, add your dried herbs and gently work the dough kneading it for 3-4 minutes. Place your dough back into your bowl (lightly flour the bowl to prevent sticking later) cling film the bowl and leave in a warm area for around an hour or doubled in size.

Lightly flour your work surface and now with your risen dough you are going to remove from the bowl and stretch your mix with your hands or a rolling pin, place the dough into your lightly greased roasting tin and massage the dough to ensure it fills the whole dish leaving it looking dimply, cover again and leave for another 30 minutes.

Once it has started to rise again you can season with salt and pepper and drizzle the remaining oil over your dough, massage again leaving it looking dimply and rustic.

Place into your preheated oven for 25-30 minutes.

I normally like to sprinkle some fresh herbs and a light sprinkling of cheese just before its finished and literally flash in the oven for 2 minutes to infuse the fresh herbs into the finished bread.

Serve fresh or gently warm through in the oven later when you require it.

PIZZA DOUGH

You will need

250g bread flour
2 teaspoons salt
2 teaspoons sugar
2 teaspoons of yeast
2 tablespoons olive oil
Some warm water
Or

250g plain flour
2 teaspoons of baking powder
2 teaspoons of sugar
2 teaspoons of salt
2 tablespoons of olive oil
Some warm water

A mixing bowl
A rolling pin
A lined baking tray or pizza tray if you have one.
Preheat oven 180C/GM4

For your sauce you can either use a tomato purée base or swap it for a pesto or sun dried tomato pesto or use a jar of pasta sauce if you have one in the cupboard.

The simplest recipe and you'll love it, sieve your flour, add your other dry ingredients and your olive oil and combine together.

Slowly start to add your warm water and continue to mix until you've formed a firm dough gently knead the dough for a few minutes.

With your hands or a rolling pin on a floured work surface roll out your dough to a circular shape that will fit onto your baking tray or pizza dish.

Cover and leave for 10 minutes.

That's it, all you need to do is build your pizza, tomato base or garlic butter and then create your favourite.

Toppings .... anything you like.... need to get rid of stuff in the fridge use it here ... roasted vegetables ... the half pack of ham ... the odd mushroom kicking about.

The cheese .... ideally use grated mozzarella or balled mozzarella is fine ..... if you only have cheddar lurking in the fridge ... par-bake your base, plain without the sauce for 10 minutes as cheddar will turn fatty for the full bake and not look very pretty for the end result.

Festive ideas and preparation

CHRISTMAS FRUIT CAKE

TIME TO START THINKING ABOUT CHRISTMAS CAKE ..... yeah I know .... where has the year gone

Let us get that festive smell around the house to brighten our day.

You will need

1kg mixed dried fruit (use a mix of raisins, sultanas, currants, cherries, cranberries)
zest and juice 1 orange
zest and juice 1 lemon
150ml brandy, port, whisky or rum, plus extra for feeding
250g pack butter, softened
200g light soft brown sugar
275g plain flour
½ tsp baking powder
2 tsp mixed spice
1 tsp ground cinnamon
¼ tsp ground cloves
4 large eggs
1 tsp vanilla extract

A large bowl for soaking fruit
A large mixing bowl
A mixing spoon
A 20cm round or square cake tin

On the cooking day pre heat your oven 150C/GM2

Put 1kg mixed dried fruit, the zest and juice of 1 orange and 1 lemon, 150ml brandy or other alcohol

And leave overnight to absorb.

The next day in a large saucepan add the following

250g softened butter and 200g light, soft brown sugar and your soaked fruit set over a medium heat on your stove stirring continuously

Up your heat just a little more to gently bring to the boil, then lower the heat and simmer for 5 minutes. Tip the fruit mixture into a large bowl and leave to cool for 30 minutes.

Heat oven to 150C/GM 2. Line a deep 20cm cake tin with a double layer of baking parchment.

Add 275g plain flour, ½ tsp baking powder, 2 tsp mixed spice, 1 tsp ground cinnamon, ¼ tsp ground cloves, 4 large eggs and 1 tsp vanilla extract to the fruit mixture and stir well, making sure there are no pockets of flour.

Tip into your prepared tin, level the top with a spatula and bake in the centre of the oven for 2 hrs.

Remove the cake from the oven, poke holes in it with a skewer and spoon over 2 tbsp of your chosen alcohol. Leave the cake to cool completely in the tin.

To store, peel off the baking parchment, then wrap well in cling film. Feed the cake with 1-2 tablespoons of alcohol every fortnight, until you ice it.

I personally do a blend of port and brandy then on the last couple of feeds I use a cheeky bit of whiskey just give it some Christmas cheer,

Don't feed the cake for the final week to give the surface a chance to dry before icing.

MINCE PIE FILLING

You will need

600g dried mixed fruit- pre mixed or mix your own using equal amounts or currants,
sultanas & raisins
100g chopped dried cranberries
100g mixed peel - caramelised style, shop bought tub
200ml brandy
Zest and juice of 1 large orange

All the above ingredients place into a large mixing bowl and mix well, cling film the bowl
and leave to soak for 24-36 hours in a cool place stirring again half way through the
soaking time.

Right

Now this has soaked enough let's get this filling cooked.

In a large saucepan place the following ingredients

180g shredded suet (veggie)
250g soft light brown sugar
2 teaspoons of cinnamon
2 teaspoons of mixed spice

Place saucepan on a low heat and gently combine all together, then add your soaked
fruity mix and gently turn up the heat, we don't want to boil this but just bring it to a
gentle simmer and continue till you are looking at .... and smelling a beautiful
caramelised mince pie filling. Should take around 5-10 minutes.

Allow to cool for a short amount of time before placing into your sterilised jam jars,
once filled place a small disc of grease proof paper on the top of the mix of each jar
and then seal.

Store in a cool cupboard and use within 5-6 months.

CHRISTMAS COOKIES

you will need

225g soft unsalted butter or Dairy free margarine
110g caster sugar
275g plain flour
100g chopped dried cranberries
Zest of one large orange
1 teaspoon of cinnamon
1 teaspoon vanilla essence
White chocolate for melting and decorating

A mixing bowl
A sieve
A baking tray with either grease proof paper or lightly dusted with flour.

Preheat your oven to 180C/GM 4.
Sieve your flour into and the butter and gently rub the mix between your fingers to form an even crumbly mix.

Add your sugar and continue to mix until it's all evenly combined.

Start to firmly knead your mixture together to create a huge cookie dough ball at this point you can add your vanilla essence, cinnamon and orange zest to work in the flavours.

Now add your chopped dried cranberries and quickly fold this evenly into your dough mix.

Now with your mix you need to start making little balls about the size of a walnut, so tear away bits from your cookie dough and get rolling in the palm of your hands, make sure they are all equal in size, just like the chocolate chip recipe

Place these onto your greased or lined baking sheet and with two fingers gently press them down to form a nice round thickish looking biscuit just under a cm

Pop into your preheated oven and check after 10 minutes they should need around 10-15 but never forget to have a sneaky peak to see how they are doing.

Once done remove from oven and allow to cool on the tray or on a wire rack.

Melt your white chocolate either in a microwave or in a bowl over simmering water and pipe your chocolate over your cookie or dip half of it in the chocolate to make it a trendy looking cookie.

Christmas Flapjacks

You will need

320g porridge oats
80g mixed seeds (any combination of sesame, sunflower, pumpkin, hemp or linseeds)
40g dried cranberries
40g dried figs, chopped with scissors
80g raisins
1/2 tsp cinnamon
1/2 tsp ground ginger
1/4 tsp mixed spice
100ml sunflower oil
185ml honey or golden syrup

A large mixing bowl
A mixing spoon

Preheat the oven to 180C/GM 4 and line a 20x25cm tin with greaseproof paper.

Firstly as in the flapjack recipe before lightly toast off your oats and seeds in your preheated oven before starting.

Once toasted and cooled place all of the dry ingredients including your spices into a large bowl and mix well

Measure the sunflower oil and honey or golden syrup into a measuring jug. Warm in the microwave for 30 seconds before pouring over the dry ingredients. Stir well to combine.

Pour the mixture into the tin and press down well, neatening off the edge if it doesn't quite reach the end of the tin.

Bake in the oven for 20 minutes until the oats are golden. Leave to cool in the tin before turning out and cutting into 16 squares.

FESTIVE SHORTBREAD AND GINGERBREAD PERSON PARTY PLATES

YOU CAN HAVE GREAT FAMILY BAKING TIME WITH THIS PARTY FILLER USING THE SHORTBREAD RECIPE EARLIER IN THIS BOOK EITHER BATCH MAKE OR DIVIDE YOUR MIXTURE AND USING FOOD GELS RATHER THAN COLOURING LIQUIDS AS I FEEL THEY CAN AFFECT YOUR END BAKING RESULT AND DO NOT GIVE AS MUCH OF A VIBRANT FESTIVE COLOURATION IN THE END RESULT.

USING CHRISTMAS CUTTERS YOU CAN HAVE GREAT FUN DECORATING THEM WITH ICING TOO.

YOU COULD ALSO FLAVOUR THE DIFFERENT COLOURS WITH A SIMPLE ZEST OF AN ORANGE OR LEMON IN YOUR SHORTBREAD MIX WHEN YOU ARE MAKING IT.

THE SAME CAN BE DONE WITH THE GINGERBREAD PERSON RECIPE, CHANGE THE GINGER FOR A MIXED SPICE OR CINNAMON TO MAKE A LITTLE DIFFERENCE AND FILL YOUR BAKING HOUSE WITH THOSE AMAZING FESTIVE AROMAS.

YOU COULD ALSO MAKE A HOLE IN YOUR FESTIVE BISCUITS AND ONCE COOKED USING A RIBBON MAKE THEM INTO EDIBLE TREE TREATS BUT DON'T HAVE THEM HANGING ABOUT IF YOU HAVE PETS OTHERWISE YOU'LL JUST HAVE A NIGHTMARE BEFORE CHRISTMAS ON YOUR HANDS.

Basic, simple pastry recipes for all your needs

SHORTCRUST PASTRY

You will need

200g Plain Flour
100g Butter or Dairy free alternative
Pinch of salt
A splash of cold water

Sieve your Plain flour and salt and add your butter, Rub together to a an even mixture breaking down the butter with no lumps, add a splash of cold water and work the pastry quickly together. Don't over handle this mix as soon as its looking like a pastry you can form it into a rectangular block and chill or freeze until it is required.

USES
Sweet or savoury pies, quiche, tarts etc.

ROUGH PUFF PASTRY

You will need

250g Plain flour
250g Butter or Dairy free alternative (chilled)
Pinch of salt
Ice cold water

Sieve your plain flour and your pinch of salt into a mixing bowl. Roughly break 250g butter into small chunks, add them to the bowl and rub them in loosely. You need to see bits of butter.
Make a well in the bowl and pour in about two-thirds of 150ml cold water start to mix until you have a firm rough dough adding extra water if needed.
Cover with cling film and leave to rest for 20 minutes in the fridge.
Turn out onto a lightly floured board, knead gently and form into a smooth rectangle shape.
Roll the dough in one direction only, until 3 times the width, keep edges straight and even. Don't overwork the butter streaks; you should have a marbled effect.
Fold the top third down to the centre, then the bottom third up and over that. Give the dough a quarter turn (to the left or right) and roll out again to three times the length.
Once rolled form your pastry into a rectangular block, chill or freeze until needed.

USES
Sweet or savoury pies, sausage rolls, rustic party treats, cheese melts etc.

SWEET SHORTCRUST PASTRY

You will need

200g Plain flour
100g Butter or Dairy free alternative
50g icing sugar
Pinch of salt
1 egg yolk
1 teaspoon of vanilla essence

Put 150g plain flour and 75g unsalted butter in a bowl and rub together with your fingertips until it resembles breadcrumbs.
Mix in 50g icing sugar and a pinch of salt followed by 1 egg yolk and your vanilla essence. If the pastry feels too dry to form a dough, add 1 teaspoon of water to help form it together. Shape the dough into a ball, flatten it out into a disc, wrap it in cling film, chill for at least 30 minutes before using or freeze for future use.

USES
Fruit flans or tarts, mince pies, etc.

Printed in Great Britain
by Amazon

49631743R00037